Informing the legislative debate since 1914 _____

Honduras: Background and U.S. Relations

Peter J. Meyer
Analyst in Latin American Affairs

May 30, 2014

Congressional Research Service

7-5700

www.crs.gov

RL34027

Summary

Honduras, a Central American nation of 8.2 million people, has had close ties with the United States over many years. The country served as a base for U.S. operations in Central America during the 1980s, and it continues to host a U.S. military presence and cooperate on anti-drug efforts today. Trade and investment linkages are also long-standing, and have grown stronger since the implementation of the Dominican Republic-Central America-United States Free Trade Agreement (CAFTA-DR). Migration is another central concern in bilateral relations; an estimated 1 million Hondurans reside in the United States—some 600,000 of whom are believed to be undocumented. Although the U.S.-Honduras relationship was somewhat strained as a result of the 2009 political crisis in Honduras, close cooperation quickly resumed in 2010. Current U.S. policy in Honduras is focused on strengthening democratic governance, including the promotion of human rights and the rule of law, enhancing economic prosperity, and improving the long-term security situation in the country.

Political Situation

Juan Orlando Hernández, the former head of the Honduran National Congress, was inaugurated to a four-year presidential term in January 2014 after having won 37% of the vote in a four-way race in November 2013. Like his predecessor, Hernández hails from the conservative National Party. He campaigned on hardline security policies and a business-friendly platform, and has primarily focused on reducing crime and violence in the first four months of his term. Since the National Party only controls a plurality in the Honduran National Congress, Hernández will need to secure support from other parties in order to enact his legislative agenda.

Security and Human Rights

Hernández is charged with turning around a poor security and human rights situation. Honduras has the highest homicide rate in the world, and common crime is widespread. Moreover, human rights abuses—which increased in the aftermath of the country's 2009 political crisis—have persisted. A number of inter-related factors have likely contributed to this situation, including the increasing presence of organized crime, weak government institutions, and widespread corruption. Although the Honduran government has adopted some policy reforms designed to address these challenges in recent years, conditions have yet to show much improvement.

Economic and Social Conditions

Honduras also faces considerable economic and social challenges. Although the economy has partially recovered since contracting in 2009, the Honduran government's budget deficit has widened, reaching an estimated 7.6% of gross domestic product in 2013. As it has struggled to obtain financing for the budget, public employees and contractors occasionally have gone unpaid and basic government services have been interrupted. Honduras also continues to face significant social disparities, with over two-thirds of the population living in poverty.

Congressional Action

Members of Congress have expressed considerable interest in Honduras since the 2009 political crisis, focusing in particular on the state of the country's democratic institutions as well as the significant security and human rights challenges that have plagued the country in recent years. Congress has placed human rights restrictions on security assistance to Honduras since FY2012.

The Consolidated Appropriations Act, 2014 (P.L. 113-76) modifies the previous restrictions by increasing the amount of assistance that must be withheld from 20% to 35%, adding new conditions that must be met, and broadening the exemption so that the withholding requirement does not apply to border security funding. The legislation also recommends providing $1 million to support a U.N. High Commissioner on Human Rights office in Honduras.

Contents

Figures

Tables

Contacts

Political Situation

Background

Honduras, a Central American nation of 8.2 million people,[1] has struggled with political instability and authoritarian governance for much of its history. The military has traditionally played a large role in domestic politics, and essentially controlled the national government from 1963 until 1971, and again from 1972 until 1982. Hondurans elected a national constituent assembly to draft a new constitution in 1980, and the country returned to civilian rule in 1982 following presidential and legislative elections.

Even after the return to electoral democracy, the military continued to operate as an autonomous institution. While Honduras did not experience a civil conflict like those in neighboring El Salvador, Guatemala, and Nicaragua, the Honduran military pursued hardline anticommunist security policies and was responsible for human rights abuses in the 1980s. According to the National Commission for Human Rights, an independent office of the Honduran government, security forces systematically engaged in arbitrary detentions, torture, and extrajudicial executions, disappearing at least 179 people between 1980 and 1992.[2] During the 1990s, successive Honduran administrations took steps to reduce the power of the military. Mandatory military service was abolished, the police and several state-owned enterprises were removed from military control, and—after the ratification of constitutional reforms in 1999—the military was subordinated to a civilian-appointed defense minister.

The Liberal (*Partido Liberal*, PL) and National (*Partido Nacional*, PN) Parties have dominated Honduran politics since the transition to electoral democracy. Both political parties are considered to be ideologically center-right; however, the PL has historically had a small center-left wing. The parties are oriented around personalist factions and are largely viewed as vehicles for patronage.[3] According to a number of analysts, "the objective of political competition between the two parties has not been a competition for policies or programs, but rather a competition for personal gain in which the public sector is turned into private benefit."[4]

---

[1] United Nations Economic Commission for Latin America and the Caribbean (ECLAC), *Statistical Yearbook for Latin America and the Caribbean, 2013*, December 2013, p.33, http://www.eclac.org/publicaciones/xml/5/51945/AnuarioEstadistico2013.pdf (Hereinafter: ECLAC, December 2013).

[2] Comisionado Nacional de los Derechos Humanos (CONADEH), *Los Hechos Hablan por Sí Mismos: Informe Preliminar sobre los Desaparecidos en Honduras, 1980-1993*, Second Edition, Tegucigalpa, Honduras, May 2002. An English language translation is available at http://www.cja.org/downloads/Honduras_Report-_%22The_Facts_Speak_for_Themselves%22.pdf.

[3] J. Mark Ruhl, "Honduras Unravels," *Journal of Democracy*, vol. 21, no. 2 (April 2010).

[4] *Honduras: A Country Study*, ed. Tim L. Merrill, 3rd ed. (Washington, DC: Library of Congress, Federal Research Division, 1995), p.174. Several more recent studies of the Honduran party system offer similar analysis. See, for example, Ramón Romero, "Los Partidos Políticos y el Estado Hondureño: Evidencias de la Miopía Partidaria," in *Golpe de Estado: Partidos, Instituciones, y Cultura Política* (Tegucigalpa: Centro de Documentación de Honduras, 2010), pp. 23-54 (Hereinafter: Romero 2010); and Leticia Salomón, "Honduras: Golpe de Estado, Sistema de Partidos y Recomposición Democrática," in *Honduras: Retos y Desafíos de la Reconstrucción Democrática* (Tegucigalpa: Centro de Documentación de Honduras, 2011), pp. 1-22.

Figure 1. Map of Honduras

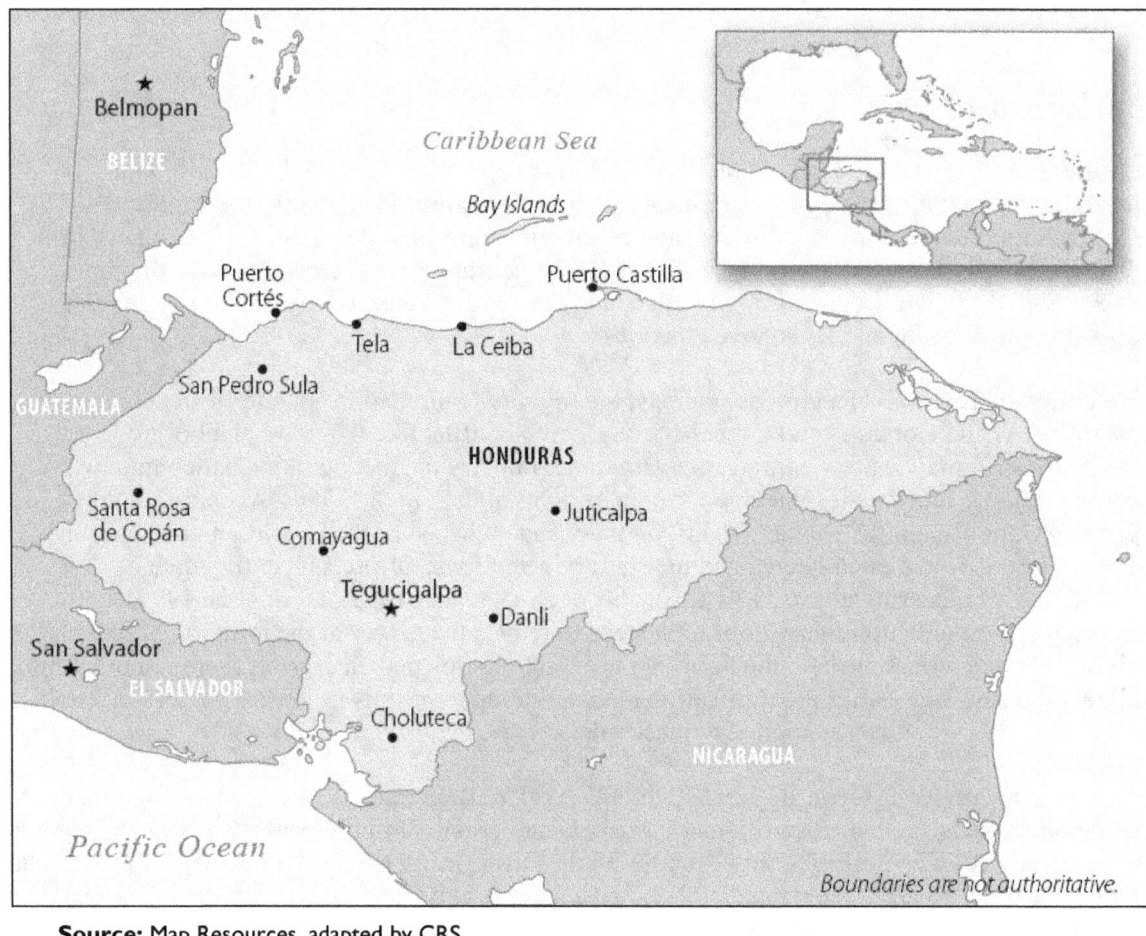

Source: Map Resources, adapted by CRS.

2009 Political Crisis[5]

Honduras was thrown into political crisis on June 28, 2009, when the Honduran military arrested then-President Manuel Zelaya and flew him into forced exile. Honduran government institutions had become increasingly polarized in the preceding months as Zelaya—who was elected as a relatively moderate member of the PL—pursued a series of populist measures and called for a new constitution. The ouster was ultimately triggered by Zelaya's determination to push ahead with a non-binding referendum[6] on the possibility of constitutional reform despite judicial orders forbidding it. Although the majority of the Honduran National Congress and Supreme Court backed Zelaya's removal, Zelaya was never given due process and the Truth and Reconciliation

---

[5] For a more detailed examination of the Honduran political crisis, see CRS Report R41064, *Honduran Political Crisis, June 2009-January 2010*.

[6] The non-binding referendum would have asked Hondurans, "Do you agree that in the general elections of 2009, a fourth ballot box should be installed in which the people decide on the convocation of a National Constituent Assembly?" "Llegó el Día de Verdad," *El Tiempo* (Honduras), June 28, 2009.

Commission appointed to investigate the ouster (along with most other legal and political analysts) declared it a "coup d'état."[7]

The Honduran National Congress named Roberto Micheletti, the head of Congress and a member of a more conservative faction of the PL, president of Honduras for the remaining seven months of Zelaya's term.[8] While steadfastly opposing international pressure to restore Zelaya to office, Micheletti worked with the Honduran National Congress to annul a number of reforms that had been approved under Zelaya. Micheletti also maintained tight control of Honduran society, restricting the activities of those opposed to the ouster. According to the Inter-American Commission on Human Rights (IACHR), an autonomous body of the Organization of American States (OAS), serious violations of human rights occurred during the Micheletti government, including deaths, suppression of public demonstrations through disproportionate use of force, arbitrary detentions of thousands of persons, serious and arbitrary restrictions on the right to freedom of expression, and grave violations of political rights.[9] Although some sectors of Honduran society strongly supported the coup and Micheletti, polling suggests that the majority of Hondurans did not.[10]

Lobo Administration (2010-2014)

President Porfirio Lobo, elected in a November 2009 presidential election that occurred during the country's political crisis, took office in January 2010.[11] He was able to advance much of his policy agenda over the course of his four-year term since his party, the PN, controlled 71 of the 128 seats in the unicameral Honduran National Congress. However, Lobo struggled throughout his term to resolve Honduras's major challenges. While initiatives such as the creation of a truth commission and an agreement to allow former President Zelaya to return to the country won support from the international community and initially restored a measure of stability to Honduras, they were less successful in strengthening democratic institutions and rebuilding confidence in the political system.[12] In December 2012, for example, the National Congress replaced four members of the Supreme Court who had declared several recently enacted laws unconstitutional. Although the Honduran Minister of Justice and Human Rights asserted the move was illegal and threatened the independence of the judiciary, it was never overturned.[13] The Lobo Administration also achieved few concrete results in its efforts to reduce persistently high levels of crime, violence, unemployment, and poverty (see "Security and Human Rights Conditions" and "Economic and Social Conditions" below). In a December 2013 poll, over 67% of Hondurans

---

[7] Comisión de la Verdad y la Reconciliación, *Para que los Hechos No se Repitan: Informe de la Comisión de la Verdad y la Reconciliación*, San José, Costa Rica, July 2011. Also see: Edmundo Orellana, "El 28 de Junio y la Constitución," *La Tribuna* (Honduras), August 1, 2009; and Tim Johnson, "All Parties Broke Law in Honduras Coup, Envoy Wrote," *McClatchy Newspapers*, November 28, 2010.

[8] "El Decreto de la Separación de Zelaya," *El Heraldo* (Honduras), June 28, 2009.

[9] Inter-American Commission on Human Rights (IACHR), *Honduras: Human Rights and the Coup D'état*, December 30, 2009, http://cidh.org/countryrep/Honduras09eng/Toc htm.

[10] See, for example, Orlando J. Pérez, José René Argueta, and Mitchell A. Seligson, *Cultura Política de la Democracia en Honduras, 2010*, Vanderbilt University, Latin American Public Opinion Project (LAPOP), October 2010.

[11] Lobo defeated former Vice President Elvin Santos of the PL, 57% to 38%.

[12] In December 2013, roughly 75% of Hondurans reported having little or no confidence in Honduran political parties, the central government, the National Congress, and the Supreme Court. Equipo de Reflexión, Investigación y Comunicación, Compañía de Jesús (ERIC-SJ), *Percepciones Sobre la Situación Hondureña en el Año 2013*, January 2014, p.17 (Hereinafter: ERIC-SJ, January 2014).

[13] "Se Conculcó Principio de Independencia," *El Heraldo* (Honduras), December 18, 2012

---

asserted that the Lobo Administration had done little or nothing to address the demands of the population.[14]

2013 Election

On November 24, 2013, Honduras held general elections for the presidency, all 128 seats in the unicameral National Congress, 20 seats in the Central American Parliament, and nearly 2,700 municipal offices in 298 municipalities. These were the first elections held in Honduras since the controversial 2009 vote that took place during the country's political crisis. President Lobo was constitutionally ineligible to seek reelection.

Results

Juan Orlando Hernández of the ruling, conservative PN won the presidential election with 36.9% of the vote. He was followed by Xiomara Castro of the left-leaning Liberty and Re-foundation (*Libertad y Refundación*, LIBRE) party at 28.8%, Mauricio Villeda of the center-right PL at 20.3%, Salvador Nasralla of the Anti-Corruption Party (*Partido Anticorrupción*, PAC) at 13.4%, and four other candidates that split 0.6% of the vote.[15]

Figure 2. Party Affiliation in the Honduran National Congress

Seat Distribution following the 2009 and 2013 Elections

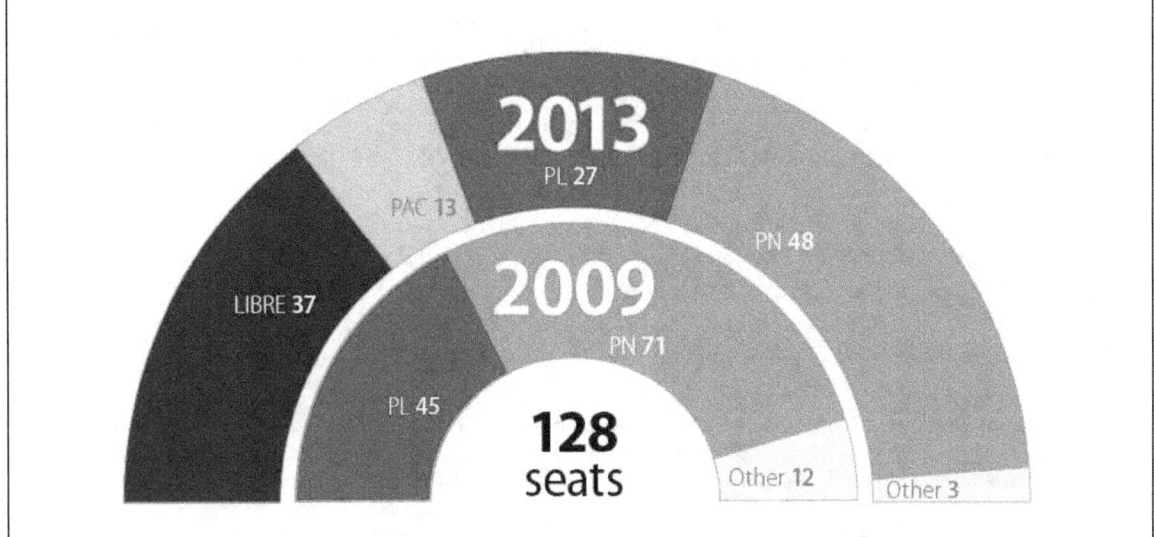

Source: Prepared by Amber Hope Wilhelm, CRS Graphics Specialist.

Notes: The Honduran National Congress is unicameral.

The PN also won a plurality in the unicameral National Congress, taking 48 of 128 seats. The new Congress is much more fragmented than its predecessor, however, as LIBRE and the PAC

---

[14] ERIC-SJ, January 2014, op. cit., p.15.

[15] Tribunal Supremo Electoral, "Resultado Presidencial," accessed December 2013, http://siede.tse hn/escrutinio/presidente.php.

have established themselves as significant opposition forces, respectively winning 37 and 13 seats in their first elections. The PL won 27 seats, and three minor parties each won a single seat in the National Congress (see **Figure 2**).[16]

The results of the election suggest that Honduras's traditional two-party system, dominated by the PL and PN, has fractured. While Hondurans' ties to the PL and PN had been weakening for years as a result of the traditional parties' failure to adequately address citizens' most pressing concerns, the 2009 political crisis appears to have been a tipping point for the two-party system. In the aftermath of the coup, many Hondurans that previously supported the PL joined Zelaya in leaving the party and founding LIBRE. Others have been willing to leave the PL and PN behind for new parties like the PAC.

Legitimacy

The U.S. government and several international observation missions consider the elections to have been generally free and fair.[17] Whereas some candidates and sectors of the population boycotted the 2009 elections due to the coup and government-imposed restrictions on civil liberties during the campaign period, the full ideological spectrum participated in the 2013 elections. The observation missions maintain that the campaign was largely peaceful, with candidates and parties able to assemble, express themselves, and travel freely. Election Day was observed by more than 700 international election observers and 7,500 Hondurans.[18] According to the observation missions, voting proceeded with few problems. More than 61% of Honduras's 5.4 million registered voters cast ballots,[19] producing the largest turnout since 2001. The observation missions also assert that the vote tabulation process was largely transparent; representatives from the three largest parties (PN, PL, and LIBRE) were present in at least 95% of observed voting places.[20]

At the same time, observers have highlighted some problems with the elections. Several organizations documented threats and attacks against candidates and political activists during the campaign period, including at least 23 murders between May 2012 and July 2013.[21] Some observers also criticized the opaque and unequal financing of the elections. Other alleged

---

[16] "Honduras: Hernández Takes Office," *Latin American Weekly Report*, January 30, 2014.

[17] Embassy of the United States Tegucigalpa Honduras, "Statement by Secretary Kerry on Honduras Elections," Press Release, December 12, 2013; OAS, "Preliminary Report of the Electoral Observation Mission of the OAS in Honduras," Press Release, December 19, 2013, http://www.oas.org/en/media_center/press_release.asp?sCodigo=E-490/13. (Hereinafter: OAS, December 2013). European Union (EU) Election Observation Mission, Honduras 2013, *Final Report on the General Elections*, 2014, http://www.eueom.eu/files/pressreleases/english/final-report-eueom-honduras-2013_en.pdf (Hereinafter: EU, 2014).

[18] EU, 2014, op. cit., p.22.

[19] Tribunal Supremo Electoral, "Resumen de Resultados," accessed May 2014, http://siede.tse hn/app.php/divulgacionmonitoreo/reporte-presidente.

[20] EU, 2014, op. cit; OAS, December 2013, op. cit.

[21] Universidad Nacional Autonoma de Honduras (UNAH), Instituto Universitario en Democracia, Paz y Seguridad (IUDPAS) and National Democratic Institute (NDI), *Boletín Informativo de la Conflictividad y Violencia Político Electoral*, October 2013. Another study documented 35 murders of candidates, activists, or family members between May 2012 and October 19, 2013. See: Karen Spring, *Context of the Honduran Electoral Process 2012-2013: Incomplete List of Killings and Armed Attacks Related to Political Campaigning in Honduras, May 2012 to October 19, 2013*, Rights Action, October 21, 2013, http://rightsaction.org/sites/default/files/Honduras-Violence-Political-Campaign.pdf.

---

irregularities included eligible voters who were purged from the rolls, and the buying and selling of votes and polling place credentials.[22]

LIBRE and the PAC both alleged that the elections had been marred by fraud, and that some of the vote tallies changed between being counted at polling places and being recorded in the Supreme Electoral Tribunal's (*Tribunal Supremo Electoral*, TSE) official figures. LIBRE took its case to the Honduran Supreme Court but the Court rejected the party's appeal. *Hagamos Democracia*—a consortium of Honduran organizations receiving technical assistance from the National Democratic Institute (NDI)—conducted a so-called "quick count" on Election Day in an attempt to verify the official results. Using a statistically random sample of actual polling station vote tallies, *Hagamos Democracia* projected a result that was within one point of the official TSE result for each presidential candidate.[23] Nevertheless, nearly 49% of Hondurans polled in December 2013 thought there had been electoral fraud.[24]

Hernández Administration (2014-Present)

President Juan Orlando Hernández was inaugurated on January 27, 2014, and is now four months into his four-year term. Having campaigned on a hardline security platform, Hernández has primarily focused on reducing crime and violence. Since taking office, he has ordered the recently created military police force into the streets of the capital, pushed ahead with a plan—opposed by the U.S. government—to allow the Honduran military to shoot down civilian aircraft suspected of engaging in illicit activities, and overseen the first ever extradition of a Honduran citizen to the United States. These early actions have won Hernández considerable popular support. According to a May 2014 poll, 66% of Hondurans approve of Hernández's job in office.[25]

Hernández may encounter more challenges enacting the rest of his agenda. Since the PN only controls a plurality of the Honduran National Congress, Hernández must reach out to other parties in order to pass legislation (see **Figure 2**). While the PN was able to secure control of the leadership of the National Congress with support from the PL, a disputed municipal election has strained relations between the two traditional parties.[26] Hernández is unlikely to find much support among other parties in the National Congress since the PAC and LIBRE have formed an opposition bloc, and those parties' leaders reportedly have accused the Hernández Administration of governing in an authoritarian manner.[27]

---

[22] EU, 2014, op. cit; Federación International de Derechos Humanos, *Misión Internacional de la Federación International de Derechos Humanos con Apoyo de CIPRODEH sobre Elecciones en Honduras*, November 25, 2013.

[23] With a reported margin of error of 2.2%, *Hagamos Democracia* projected that Hernández would win 36% of the vote, and would be followed by Castro (28%), Villeda (21%), Nasralla (14%), and the others (0.8%). Hagamos Democracia, *Informe de Hagamos Democracia*, November 24, 2013.

[24] ERIC-SJ, January 2014, op. cit., p.7.

[25] "Reducir la Delincuencia, el Mayor Logro del Presidente de Honduras," *La Prensa* (Honduras), May 27, 2014.

[26] "Crisis Over San Luis Election Threatens Bigger Rift," *Economist Intelligence Unit*, May 6, 2014.

[27] "Salvador Nasralla: 'PAC Exigirá Representante en el Tribunal Electoral," *La Tribuna* (Honduras), May 17, 2014; "Militares Desalojan en Honduras a Ex Presidente Zelaya y Partidarios del Congreso," *Reuters*, May 14, 2014.

Security and Human Rights Conditions

Honduras has long struggled to address high levels of crime and violence, but the deterioration in security conditions has accelerated in recent years. Homicide rates rose rapidly, from an already high 31 murders per 100,000 residents in 2004 to 86.5 murders per 100,000 residents in 2011 (see **Figure 3**). While the homicide rate has declined over the past two years, falling to 79 per 100,000 residents in 2013,[28] Honduras continues to have the highest homicide rate in the world.[29] Common crime is also widespread. In a December 2013 poll, nearly 26% of Hondurans reported they had been the victim of a crime in the past year.[30] Moreover, the deteriorating security situation has taken a toll on the Honduran economy. The World Bank estimates that crime and violence cost the country the equivalent of 10% of gross domestic product (GDP) annually.[31]

Figure 3. Homicide Rate in Honduras: 2004-2013

Homicides per 100,000 residents

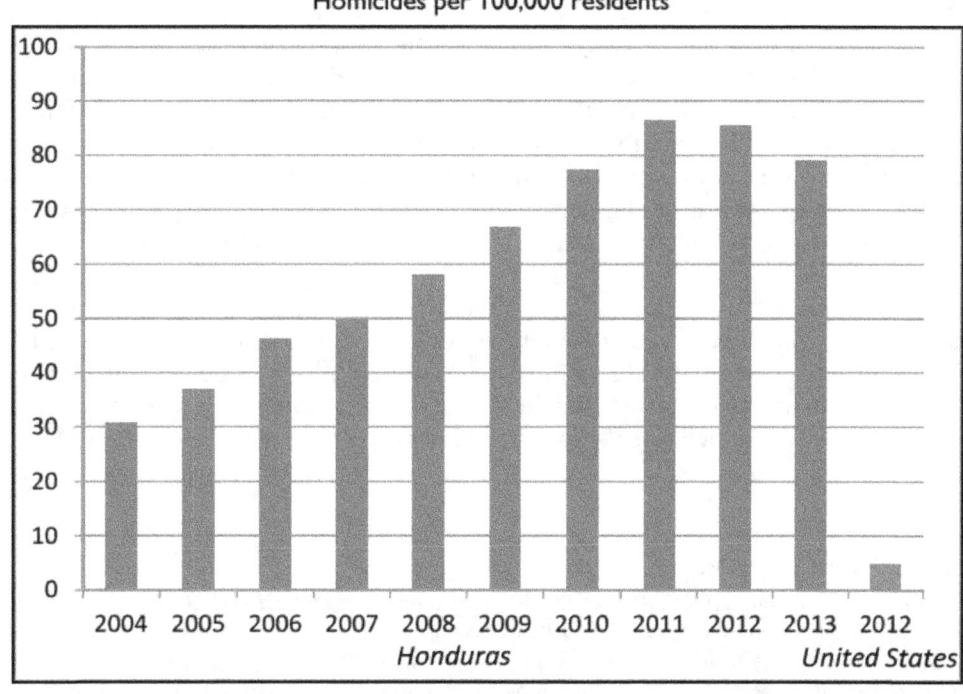

Source: CRS presentation of data from Universidad Nacional Autonoma de Honduras, Observatorio de la Violencia. U.S. homicide data, provided as a point of comparison, from the Federal Bureau of Investigation (FBI).

Many observers have been particularly concerned by a surge in violence against journalists and political and social activists. The frequency of such attacks increased in the aftermath of the June 2009 ouster of then-President Zelaya, and the attacks have continued in the years since then. At least 35 members of the media have been killed in Honduras since 2010.[32] Many others have been

---

[28] UNAH, Observatorio de la Violencia, *Boletín Nacional, Edición No.32 (Enero – Diciembre 2013)*, February 2014.

[29] United Nations Office on Drugs and Crime (UNODC), *Global Study on Homicide 2013: Trends, Contexts, Data*, March 2014, http://www.unodc.org/documents/gsh/pdfs/2014_GLOBAL_HOMICIDE_BOOK_web.pdf.

[30] ERIC-SJ, January 2014, op. cit., p.16.

[31] World Bank, "Honduras Overview," April 10, 2014.

[32] CONADEH, "Entre Noviembre 2003/Abril 2014: En la Impunidad 90% de los 42 Periodistas y Comunicadores (continued...)

threatened, harassed, or attacked, with those who report on sensitive issues such as drug trafficking, government corruption, and land conflicts being the most frequent targets.[33] In the *Bajo Aguan* region of Honduras, the site of a long-running land conflict, at least 57 individuals that were affiliated with, or sympathized with, land rights activists were killed between September 2009 and March 2013.[34] Likewise, at least 31 trade unionists have been killed in Honduras since 2009.[35] Most of these cases have never been thoroughly investigated.

Criminal Threats, Weak Institutions, and Corruption

A number of inter-related factors have likely contributed to the worsening security and human rights situation. One aspect is the increasing presence of organized crime. An estimated 12,000 Honduran youth have ties to the *Mara Salvatrucha* (MS-13) and the "18th Street" gang (M-18).[36] These organizations engage in a wide variety of criminal activities, including kidnapping and extortion.[37] Honduras also serves as an important drug trafficking corridor as a result of its location between cocaine-producing countries in South America and the major consumer market in the United States. U.S.-backed security efforts over the past two decades have restricted trafficking through the Caribbean, weakened Colombian cartels, and disrupted direct shipping to Mexico. Consequently, Mexican criminal organizations (such as the *Sinaloa* cartel and *Los Zetas*) and local affiliates are now battling for control of Central American territory.[38] Many of the most violent municipalities in Honduras are along strategic drug trafficking corridors (see **Figure 4**). Given that more than two-thirds of Hondurans live below the poverty line,[39] a large portion of the population could be susceptible to recruitment by these and other criminal groups.

Institutional weaknesses and corruption in the Honduran government have also contributed to deteriorating security and human rights conditions. In 2012, the Honduran police force had about 12,800 personnel and a budget of $163 million (0.9% of GDP)[40]—a force strength and resources that analysts maintain are "grossly insufficient for the efficient policing of a country the size of Honduras."[41] In 2013, the police force's investigative body (*Dirección Nacional de Investigación*

(...continued)

Sociales Muertos Violentamente," May 25, 2014.

[33] Committee to Protect Journalists (CPJ), *Attacks on the Press: Journalism on the Front Lines in 2013*, 2014, https://cpj.org/2014/02/attacks-on-the-press-in-2013-honduras.php.

[34] IACHR, *Annual Report of the Inter-American Commission on Human Rights 2013*, April 2014, p.441, http://www.oas.org/en/iachr/docs/annual/2013/docs-en/AnnualReport-Chap4-Honduras.pdf (Hereinafter: IACHR, 2014).

[35] American Center for International Labor Solidarity, "Central American Trade Unionists Increasingly Targeted," February 3, 2014.

[36] UNODC, *Transnational Organized Crime in Central America and the Caribbean: A Threat Assessment*, September 2012, http://www.unodc.org/documents/data-and-analysis/Studies/TOC_Central_America_and_the_Caribbean_english.pdf. (Hereinafter: UNODC, September 2012).

[37] For more information, see CRS Report RL34112, *Gangs in Central America*, by Clare Ribando Seelke.

[38] Patrick Corcoran, "Mexican Cartels Expand into Honduras," *InSight Crime*, April 14, 2011; UNODC, September 2012, op. cit.

[39] ECLAC, December 2013, op. cit..

[40] Red de Seguridad y Defensa de América Latina (RESDAL), *Public Security Index, Central America: Costa Rica, El Salvador, Guatemala, Honduras, Nicaragua and Panama*, 2013.

[41] "Country Risk Assessment: Honduras," *IHS Jane's Defense and Security Intelligence and Analysis*, February 8, 2012.

Criminal, DNIC) asserted that it had insufficient resources to investigate every crime, and that each agent had a backlog of over 460 pending cases.[42] The police force also suffers from widespread corruption, with analysts asserting that some officers have moved beyond taking bribes or tipping off criminals to actually participating in crimes and acting as enforcers for criminal interests.[43] Moreover, recent press investigations suggest that corruption and criminality may run to the very top of the organization.[44] Some 72% of Hondurans report having little or no confidence in the police force.[45]

Partially as a result of the serious flaws in the police force, Honduran presidents have repeatedly turned to the armed forces to provide internal security. The Honduran military, however, has its own limitations. In 2012, Honduras had roughly 10,600 military personnel, and a defense budget of $189 million (1% of GDP). The Honduran military is almost entirely dependent on international donors for functioning equipment and technology since less than 2% of the defense budget is invested in maintenance and procurement.[46] Corruption is also a problem. The military has been linked to drug trafficking in Honduras since the 1980s,[47] and recent reports suggest some sectors continue to engage in illicit activities.[48] Although the military is more respected than the police force, over 59% of Hondurans report having little or no confidence in the armed forces.[49]

Other justice sector institutions are prone to similar problems. In 2013, Honduras's Attorney General asserted that the Public Ministry only has the capacity to investigate 20% of the homicides that occur in Honduras.[50] Although most criminals are never brought to justice, the Honduran prison system is overcrowded. Honduras's hardline anti-gang laws make it relatively easy to detain suspected gang members, but the judiciary is incapable of dealing with the volume of cases.[51] Honduran prisons, which have capacity for about 8,600 inmates, held nearly 13,000 prisoners as of September 2013—only 50% of whom had been sentenced.[52]

---

[42] "Unos 60 Mil Homicidios sin Resolver Tienen los Cuerpos de Investigación," *El Heraldo* (Honduras), February 20, 2013.

[43] Edward Fox, "Dynamics of Honduran Police Corruption Narrow Chance for Reform," *InSight Crime*, January 31, 2012; Diego Jiménez, "'El Incendio en Comayagua Evidencia el Colapso del Sistema,'" *La Nación* (Costa Rica), February 26, 2012.

[44] Frances Robles, "Graft, Greed, Mayhem Turn Honduras into Murder Capital of World," *Miami Herald*, January 22, 2012; Daniel Valencia Caravantes, "Así es la Policía del País Más Violento del Mundo," *El Faro* (El Salvador), March 19, 2012; Charles Parkinson, "At Least 4 Top Honduras Cops Lead Drug Trafficking Rings: NGO," *InSight Crime*, January 29, 2014.

[45] ERIC-SJ, January 2014, op. cit., p.17.

[46] RESDAL, *Atlas Comparativo de la Defensa en América Latina y Caribe*, 2012.

[47] Mark B. Rosenberg, "Narcos and Politicos: Politics of Drug Trafficking in Honduras," *Journal of Interamerican Studies and World Affairs*, Vol. 30, No. 2/3, (Summer-Autumn 1988).

[48] Geoffrey Ramsey, "Cable: Honduran Military Supplied Weaponry to Cartels," *InSight Crime*, April 25, 2011; "In Brief – Honduras: Soldiers Done for Munitions Theft," *Latin News Daily Report*, June 26, 2012; and "Condenados en Honduras 13 Militares por Robo de Avioneta Decomisada a Narcos," *Agence France Presse*, June 26, 2013.

[49] ERIC-SJ, January 2014, op. cit., p.17.

[50] "Ministerio Público Solo Tiene Capacidad para Investigar 20% de Homicidios: Rubí," *La Prensa* (Honduras), April 10, 2013.

[51] Hannah Stone, "Honduras Prison Fire Tells of Repressive Anti-Gang Policies," *InSight Crime*, February 16, 2012.

[52] U.S. Department of State, Bureau of Democracy, Human Rights and Labor, *Country Reports on Human Rights Practices for 2013*, p.4, February 27, 2014, http://www.state.gov/documents/organization/220663.pdf.

This lack of capacity and susceptibility to corruption goes well beyond the security forces and justice sector. The patronage system, which allows the political parties to place their supporters in government positions after each election, has prevented the development of a professional civil service. As a result, Honduran officials often lack technical expertise and rarely engage in long-term strategic planning.[53] Likewise, Honduras ranks near the bottom of the Western Hemisphere in Transparency International's annual *Corruption Perceptions Index*, suggesting public-sector corruption is relatively widespread.[54] This apparently includes infiltration by organized crime. Shortly before being assassinated in December 2011, Alfredo Landaverde—a well-respected anti-corruption advocate and former head of Honduras's Anti-Narcotics Commission—asserted that 10% of the members of the Honduran National Congress were involved in drug-trafficking.[55]

Public Security Policies

Recent Honduran presidents have implemented varying anti-crime strategies, but none of them have achieved much success. During his term, President Ricardo Maduro (2002-2006) increased the size of the police force, sent the military into the streets, and implemented hardline anti-gang policies that made membership illegal and punishable with 12 years in prison. Although the crackdown won popular support and initially reduced crime, its success was short-lived. President Zelaya (2006-2009) replaced the previous administration's zero-tolerance policy with dialogue and other efforts to reintegrate gang members into society. Failure to achieve concrete results, however, led the Zelaya Administration to shift its emphasis toward more traditional law enforcement operations. The deterioration in security conditions accelerated in the aftermath of Zelaya's ouster, as Roberto Micheletti (2009-2010) reoriented the security forces away from combating organized crime to controlling the population.[56] President Lobo (2010-2014) heavily relied on the military to provide public security throughout his term, but also enacted a number of legal reforms and initiated some efforts to reform security and justice sector institutions. President Hernández, who helped enact many of the Lobo Administration's policies as head of the National Congress, has continued his predecessor's hardline approach to security thus far.

Institutional Reform

In recent years, the Honduran government has enacted significant changes to the country's legal framework. These include a law against terrorism finance; a reform to allow 48-hour detentions; regulations to allow asset forfeiture and wiretapping; and a constitutional amendment to allow the extradition of Honduran citizens in cases of drug trafficking, organized crime, and terrorism. The Honduran government also increased taxes on certain industries in order to provide more funding

---

[53] Romero, 2010, op. cit.

[54] On a scale of 0 (the country is perceived as highly corrupt) to 100 (the country is perceived as very clean), Honduras receives a score of 29. Transparency International, *Corruption Perceptions Index 2013*, December 2013, http://www.transparency.org/cpi2013/.

[55] Just days before he was assassinated, Landaverde appeared on a television program and stated that he had a list of Honduran officials tied to organized crime and drug-trafficking. Tim Johnson, "Drug Gangs Muscle into New Territory: Central America," *McClatchy Newspapers*, April 21, 2011.

[56] James Bosworth, *Honduras: Organized Crime Gaining Amid Political Crisis*, Woodrow Wilson International Center for Scholars, Working Paper Series on Organized Crime in Central America, December 2010, http://www.wilsoncenter.org/sites/default/files/Bosworth.FIN.pdf.

for security efforts. The tax package was partially rolled back, however, as a result of fierce private sector opposition.[57] Some of these legal changes are still in the process of implementation.

In reaction to a series of scandals in which the police were implicated in murders and other criminal activities, Honduran officials established two commissions to reform the police force and other justice sector institutions. In December 2011, the National Congress created the Directorate for the Investigation and Evaluation of the Police Career (*Dirección de Investigación y Evaluación de la Carrera Policial*, DIECP) to replace the former internal affairs unit of the police, which was reported to be rather ineffective.[58] The National Congress then established a Public Security Reform Commission (*Comisión de Reforma a la Seguridad Pública*, CRSP) in January 2012. The CRSP was empowered to investigate the police, the public prosecutor's office, and the judiciary, and suggest reforms to strengthen the institutions and reduce corruption.[59]

The commissions have produced mixed results. The DIECP was slow to begin its effort to purge the police force, but has reportedly dismissed nearly 750 officers over the past two years.[60] The CRSP carried out a series of institutional evaluations and then proposed a variety of reforms to the police, the public prosecutor's office, and the judiciary in October 2012. The Honduran Congress never acted on the proposals, however, and the outgoing Congress abolished the CRSP on the last day of its legislative session in January 2014.[61]

Use of Military

Following in the footsteps of his predecessors, President Hernández has called upon the armed forces to support internal security efforts. As the head of the Honduran National Congress in August 2013, Hernández helped create a new military police force (*Policía Militar de Orden Público*) under the control of the Ministry of Defense. Upon taking office, Hernández immediately initiated a military police operation in the capital, seeking to increase the military and police presence on the streets and on public transportation.[62] The military police force, which currently consists of 2,000 officers, is expected to grow to 5,000 officers in the coming years, and will reportedly focus on maintaining security in the most crime-ridden neighborhoods.[63]

While sending the armed forces into the streets is quite popular among Hondurans,[64] a number of analysts have raised concerns about this increasing reliance on the military for domestic security. Some assert that the military has begun to carve out a larger role for itself in internal political and economic affairs, and argue that this is a worrying trend since the military was only subordinated to civilian leadership in the late 1990s.[65] In addition to playing a leading role in the 2009 coup

---

[57] "Honduras Cuts Security Tax After Angering Businesses," *Reuters*, September 14, 2011.

[58] "Cisma en la Policía Nacional: 60 Días de Escándalos," *El Tiempo* (Honduras), December 22, 2011.

[59] "Honduras: Lobo Makes Move to Purge Police," *Latin American Weekly Report*, February 2, 2012.

[60] "Policía de Honduras ha Destituido 748 Agentes en los Últimos dos Años," *La Tribuna* (Honduras), January 22, 2014.

[61] "Honduras: Comisión Está en Deuda con Reformas a la Seguridad Pública," *El Heraldo* (Honduras), June 19, 2013; "Disuelven la CRSP y Eligen a Magistrados del TSE 6 Meses Antes," *La Prensa* (Honduras), January 20, 2014.

[62] Michael Lohmuller, "New Honduras President Sends Soldiers to Capital's Streets," *InSight Crime*, January 28, 2014.

[63] "1,000 Agentes Más a la Policía Militar," *El Heraldo* (Honduras), May 6, 2014.

[64] According to a poll released in September 2013, 77% of Hondurans agree that the military should patrol the streets. "El 77% de los Hondureños Quiere a los Militares en las Calles," *La Prensa* (Honduras), September 26, 2013.

[65] See, for example, Thelma Mejía, "Honduras: Putting Defense in the Hands of Civilians," *Inter Press Service*, (continued...)

---

against then-President Zelaya, the military reportedly surrounded the National Congress as it voted to dismiss members of the Supreme Court in December 2012,[66] and the military police reportedly appeared in campaign advertisements for President Hernández.[67] U.S. military officials have argued that utilizing the Honduran military for domestic security matters "is a necessary initial step to help curb the rising tide of violence," but maintain that such an approach "is unsustainable in the long term."[68] According to many security analysts, regional efforts to militarize law enforcement have generally failed to reduce violence and have contributed to human rights violations.[69]

Human Rights Initiatives

In addition to these security policies, the Honduran government has taken several steps designed to improve the human rights situation in Honduras. In 2010, then-President Lobo created a new Secretariat for Justice and Human Rights to promote, coordinate, and evaluate justice and human rights policies. The IACHR maintains that the Secretariat has "played an important role in public policy on human rights, having taken a number of measures to promote and protect them."[70] In January 2013, the Lobo Administration adopted a new human rights policy and plan of action that reportedly had been drafted by the Secretariat after extensive consultations with civil society. In accordance with the plan of action, the Secretariat drafted a bill designed to protect human rights defenders, journalists, social broadcasters, and operators of justice; the bill was introduced in the Honduran National Congress in August 2013.[71]

The Honduran government has also adopted many policies recommended by the international community. In November 2010, Honduras submitted to the U.N. Human Rights Council's universal periodic review process. As of May 2013, the Honduran government reportedly had completed 71 of the 129 recommendations it had received through the review, and was in the process of completing 52 others.[72] These range from ratifying various international human rights treaties to requesting that the Office of the U.N. High Commissioner on Human Rights (OHCHR) open an office in the country. The explanatory statement[73] accompanying the Consolidated Appropriations Act, 2014 (P.L. 113-76) recommends providing $1 million to support an OHCHR office in Honduras.

(...continued)

October 4, 2011; Geoffrey Ramsey, "New Powers for Honduran Military Will Not Clean Up Law Enforcement," *InSight Crime*, November 30, 2011, and Thelma Mejía, "Military Given Full Powers to Fight Crime in Honduras, *Inter Press Service*, September 4, 2013.

[66] Alberto Arce, "Flailing Honduras in Yet Another Political Crisis," *Associated Press*, December 14, 2012.

[67] Alberto Arce, "Security, Military Police Dominate Honduras Vote," *Associated Press*, November 23, 2013.

[68] General Douglas M. Fraser, United States Air Force Commander, *Posture Statement Before the 112th Congress, House Armed Services Committee*, United States Southern Command, March 6, 2012, p. 24, http://armed-services.senate.gov/statemnt/2012/03%20March/Fraser%2003-13-12.pdf.

[69] Daniela Castro, "Experts Seek End to Militarization of LatAm Policing," *InSight Crime*, September 25, 2013.

[70] IACHR, 2014, op. cit., p.467.

[71] Ibid.

[72] "Honduras Ha Cumplido Unas 71 Recomendaciones Sobre DDHH," *El Tiempo* (Honduras), May 7, 2013.

[73] The joint explanatory statement is available from the House Committee on Rules at: http://rules house.gov/bill/113/hr-3547-sa.

Human rights organizations maintain that these efforts have been insufficient. They criticize the Honduran government for repeatedly dismissing the possibility that attacks against journalists and activists might be related to the victims' professions or activism. They also criticize the Honduran government for failing to properly investigate human rights violations and bring those responsible to justice.[74] In October 2013, several members of the human rights unit of the attorney general's office were suddenly rotated to different offices. The human rights prosecutors involved maintain that they were moved for pursuing cases against influential people.[75]

Economic and Social Conditions

Honduras is a lower-middle-income developing country with an estimated GDP of $19.6 billion and an estimated per capita GDP of $2,368.[76] The Honduran economy historically has been dependent on agricultural exports such as coffee and bananas. While these commodities remain important, the Honduran economy has become more diversified since the 1990s as a result of significant growth in nontraditional sectors such as the *maquiladora*, or export-processing industry. In 1998, Honduras was devastated by Hurricane Mitch, which killed more than 5,000 people and caused billions of dollars in damage. The economy contracted by 1.9% in 1999, but rebounded with average annual growth of 5.1% between 2000 and 2008.[77] During the same time period, international financial institutions provided Honduras with $2.4 billion in debt relief to free government resources for poverty alleviation efforts.[78]

Honduras at a Glance
Land Area: 111,890 sq. km (slightly larger than Virginia)
Population: 8.2 million (2014 est.)
Race/Ethnicity: 90% *Mestizo* (mixed Amerindian and European), 7% Amerindian, 2% black, 1% white
Religions: 65% Roman Catholic, 35% Protestant
Official Language: Spanish
GDP: $19.6 billion (2014 est.)
GDP per Capita: $2,368 (2014 est.)
Top Exports: coffee, bananas, seafood, palm oil (2013)
Poverty Rate: 67.4% (2010)
Indigence Rate: 42.8% (2010)
Adult Literacy Rate: 85.1% (2011)
Life Expectancy: 72.8 years (2010-2015 est.)
Infant Mortality Rate: 23.5 per 1,000 live births (2010-2015 est.)
Sources: Area, race/ethnicity, and religion statistics from the U.S. State Department; GDP estimates from the IMF; export data from Global Trade Atlas; and population and social statistics from ECLAC.

---

[74] See, for example, Human Rights Watch, *"There Are No Investigations Here": Impunity for Killings and Other Abuses in Bajo Aguán Honduras*, February 12, 2014, http://www.hrw.org/sites/default/files/reports/honduras0214web.pdf.

[75] "Cisma y Malestar en el MP por Rotación de Fiscales," *El Heraldo* (Honduras), October 28, 2013.

[76] International Monetary Fund (IMF), *World Economic Outlook Database April 2014*, April 8, 2014.

[77] Ibid.

[78] IMF, "IMF and World Bank Support US$1 Billion in Debt Service Relief for Honduras," Press Release No. 05/76, April 5, 2005; Inter-American Development Bank (IDB), "IDB Governors Approve $4.4 Billion in Debt Relief for Bolivia, Guyana, Haiti, Honduras and Nicaragua," Press Release, March 16, 2007.

2009 Crises

As an open economy that is closely tied to the United States, Honduras is sensitive to international downturns. By early 2009, Honduras was experiencing significant declines in remittances, tourism, and export earnings as a result of the global financial crisis and U.S. recession.[79] The ouster of President Zelaya exacerbated these economic problems, as the international community, which had been expected to finance 20% of the government's budget,[80] imposed a series of economic sanctions on Honduras. International financial institutions withheld access to loans and other transfers, the European Union and United States terminated some foreign aid, and Venezuela stopped supplying the country with subsidized oil. Domestic opponents of the ouster placed additional pressure on the economy, engaging in strikes, transportation blockades, and other measures designed to paralyze economic activity. Curfews implemented by the Micheletti government to suppress demonstrations by the political opposition further inhibited economic activity as workers were unable to reach their places of employment. These external and internal shocks contributed to an economic contraction of 2.4% in 2009.[81]

Fiscal Challenges

Improved economic conditions in the United States (Honduras's main source of trade, investment, and remittances) have boosted economic growth in Honduras in recent years. Real GDP increased by an average of 3.8% between 2010 and 2012.[82] Growth decelerated to 2.6% in 2013, however, as a coffee rust outbreak began to take a toll on Honduras's top export. The Honduran economy is expected to grow by 3% in 2014.[83]

Even as the economy has returned to growth, the Honduran government's budget deficit has widened, reaching an estimated 7.6% of GDP in 2013. Weak tax collection, increasing (and non-transparent) expenditures, and losses at state-owned enterprises reportedly have all contributed to the problem.[84] General government gross debt has quickly climbed from 23% of GDP in 2008 to an estimated 45% of GDP in 2014, nearly reversing the effects of previous international debt relief initiatives.[85] As the Honduran government has struggled to obtain financing for its obligations, public employees and contractors occasionally have gone unpaid, and basic government services have been interrupted.

In December 2013, the outgoing National Congress passed a fiscal reform designed to reduce the deficit by $800 million annually. The outgoing National Congress also approved a plan to break up and partially privatize the state-controlled electricity producer, *Empresa Nacional de Energia Electrica* (ENEE), which has faced annual losses of roughly $200 million. The fiscal reform measure was partially rolled back by the newly inaugurated National Congress in January 2014,

---

[79] "Honduras: Country Report" *Economist Intelligence Unit*, April 2009.

[80] Robin Emmott, "Aid Freeze in Post-Coup Honduras Hurting Poor," *Reuters*, November 12, 2009.

[81] IMF, *World Economic Outlook Database April 2014*, April 8, 2014.

[82] Ibid.

[83] IMF, "Statement at the Conclusion of the 2014 Article IV Mission to Honduras," April 8, 2014.

[84] Ibid.; Instituto Centroamericano de Estudios Fiscales (ICEFI), *Análisis de los Compromisos y Desafíos del Nuevo Gobierno de Honduras, Presidido por Juan Orlando Hernández (Partido Nacional)*, January 27, 2014.

[85] IMF, *World Economic Outlook Database April 2014*, April 8, 2014.

---

however, as a three percentage point sales tax increase on more than 200 items in the basic consumption basket had generated widespread opposition.[86]

Poverty and Inequality

Although international debt relief initiatives and higher levels of economic growth over the past decade have allowed the Honduran government to dedicate more resources to poverty alleviation efforts, Honduras remains one of the poorest and most unequal countries in Latin America. Between 2001 and 2010, public social spending in Honduras increased from 9% of GDP to 12% of GDP.[87] During the same time period, the poverty rate fell from about 76% to 67% and the indigence rate fell from about 53% to 43%. The reduction in poverty has not been accompanied by a reduction in income disparities. The top 10% of Hondurans received 43% of all income in 2010, which is more than the bottom 80% combined and a level virtually unchanged from 2001.[88] Likewise, there continue to be significant barriers to social mobility. According to a 2012 World Bank report, only 52% of Honduran children have an equal opportunity to access basic services like timely education, running water, and electricity.[89]

U.S.-Honduras Relations

The United States has had close relations with Honduras over many years. The bilateral relationship became especially close in the 1980s when Honduras returned to civilian rule and became the lynchpin for U.S. policy in Central America. At that time, the country was a staging area for U.S.-supported excursions into Nicaragua by the *Contra* forces attempting to overthrow the leftist *Sandinista* government. Economic linkages also intensified in the 1980s after Honduras became a beneficiary of the Caribbean Basin Initiative, which provided duty-free importation of Honduran goods into the United States. Bilateral economic ties have further expanded since the entrance into force of the Dominican Republic-Central America-United States Free Trade Agreement (CAFTA-DR) in 2006.

Relations between the United States and Honduras were strained during the country's 2009 political crisis. The Obama Administration condemned the June 28 coup, and, over the course of the following months, leveled a series of diplomatic and economic sanctions designed to pressure Honduran officials to restore Zelaya to power. The Administration limited contact with the Honduran government, suspended some foreign assistance, minimized cooperation with the Honduran military, and revoked the visas of members and supporters of the Micheletti government. Micheletti reacted angrily to U.S. policy toward Honduras, reportedly declaring, "It isn't possible for anyone, no matter how powerful they are, to come over here and tell us what we have to do."[90] In November 2009, the Administration shifted the emphasis of U.S. policy from

---

[86] Gustavo Palencia, "Honduras OKs Breakup of State Power Firm, to Allow Private Investment," *Reuters*, January 20, 2014; "Congreso de Honduras Elimina Parte de Fuerte Ajuste Fiscal," *Reuters*, January 30, 2014.

[87] ECLAC, *Gasto Social en América Latina y el Caribe, Portal de Inversión Social en la Región*, January 30, 2012.

[88] ECLAC, December 2013, op. cit.

[89] José R. Molinas Vega et al., *Do Our Children Have a Chance? A Human Opportunity Report for Latin America and the Caribbean*, World Bank, Washington, DC, 2012, https://openknowledge.worldbank.org/bitstream/handle/10986/2374/656560PUB0EPI2065717B09780821386996.pdf?sequence=1.

[90] Carlos Salinas, "Honduran De Facto Leader Vows to Cling to Power Over US Objections," *El País* (Spain), August (continued...)

---

reversing Zelaya's removal to ensuring the legitimacy of previously scheduled elections. Although some analysts argued that the policy shift allowed those behind the coup to consolidate their hold on power, Administration officials maintained that elections had become the only realistic way to bring an end to the political crisis.[91]

Relations have improved considerably since 2010, when the United States restored foreign assistance and resumed cooperation with Honduras. Current U.S. policy in Honduras is focused on strengthening democratic governance, including the promotion of human rights and the rule of law, enhancing economic prosperity, and improving the long-term security situation in the country.[92] To advance these policy objectives, the United States provides Honduras with substantial amounts of foreign assistance, maintains significant security and commercial ties, and engages on transnational issues such as migration and human trafficking.

Foreign Assistance

The United States has provided significant amounts of foreign assistance to Honduras over several decades. In the 1980s, the United States provided about $2.6 billion (constant 2012 dollars) in economic and military aid to Honduras as the country supported U.S. policy objectives in the region. In the 1990s, U.S. assistance to Honduras began to wane as regional conflicts subsided and competing foreign assistance needs grew in other parts of the world. Hurricane Mitch changed that trend as the United States provided considerable amounts of aid to help the country recover from the 1998 storm. As a result of the influx of aid, total U.S. assistance to Honduras for the 1990s amounted to about $1.2 billion (constant 2012 dollars). With Hurricane Mitch funds expended by the end of 2001, U.S. foreign aid levels to Honduras again began to decline. From 2000 to 2009, total U.S. assistance to Honduras amounted to about $949 million (constant 2012 dollars).[93]

Most U.S. assistance for Honduras is provided through the State Department and the U.S. Agency for International Development (USAID), and is funded through the annual Department of State, Foreign Operations, and Related Programs appropriations measure. The State Department and USAID request bilateral assistance specifically for Honduras in the annual *Congressional Budget Justification for Foreign Operations*. Since FY2012, Honduras has received additional assistance through USAID's Office of Transition Initiatives (OTI). OTI does not request funding by country but allocates assistance to individual nations after receiving appropriations through the Transition Initiatives (TI) account. Additionally, Honduras receives a considerable amount of assistance through the Central America Regional Security Initiative (CARSI). The State Department and USAID request CARSI funding for Central America as a whole and then later allocate assistance to individual countries or regional programs. Other agencies, such as the Department of Defense (DOD), the Millennium Challenge Corporation (MCC), and the Peace Corps, have also provided assistance to Honduras in recent years.

(...continued)

5, 2009.

[91] Ginger Thompson, "U.S. Tries to Salvage Honduras Accord," *New York Times*, November 10, 2009.

[92] U.S. Department of State, Bureau of Western Hemisphere Affairs, "U.S. Relations with Honduras," Fact Sheet, March 24, 2014.

[93] These figures are actual obligations, not appropriations, from all U.S. agencies. U.S. Agency for International Development (USAID), *U.S. Overseas Loans and Grants: Obligations and Loan Authorizations, July 1, 1945-September 30, 2012*, http://gbk.eads.usaidallnet.gov/.

Table 1. U.S. Assistance to Honduras: FY2010-FY2015

In thousands of U.S. dollars

Account	FY2010	FY2011	FY2012	FY2013	FY2014 (Estimate)	FY2015 (Request)
Total Aid	**67,694**	**85,682**	**106,365**	**60,427**	**45,317**	**52,851**
Bilateral Assistance, Subtotal	50,268	56,017	57,040	51,980	41,850	48,176
DA	37,491	42,266	46,266	44,428	36,700	44,326
GHP-USAID	11,000	10,988	8,000	3,578	0	0
GHP-State	1,000	1,000	1,000	0	0	0
NADR	0	0	0	500	0	0
IMET	777	765	774	626	650	750
FMF	0	998	1,000	2,848	4,500	3,100
TI, Subtotal[a]	**0**	**0**	**4,000**	**3,660**	**NA**	**NA**
CARSI, Subtotal[b]	**13,599**	**20,967**	**34,113**	**NA**	**NA**	**NA**
ESF	5,500	7,766	16,500	NA	NA	NA
INCLE	6,585	13,201	17,613	NA	NA	NA
FMF	1,514	0	0	NA	NA	NA
DOD, Subtotal[c]	**3,827**	**8,698**	**11,212**	**4,787**	**3,467**	**4,675**
Counternarcotics (1004 & 1033)	2,357	8,500	8,236	4,787	3,467	4,675
Humanitarian (2561)	1,470	198	2,976	NA	NA	NA

Sources: Bilateral Assistance and TI data from U.S. Department of State, *Congressional Budget Justifications for Foreign Operations, Fiscal Years 2012-2015*; CARSI data from U.S. Government Accountability Office (GAO), *Central America: U.S. Agencies Considered Various Factors in Funding Security Activities, but Need to Assess Progress in Achieving Interagency Objectives*, GAO-13-771, September 25, 2013; DOD data from U.S. Department of Defense, *Reports to Congress on Foreign-Assistance Related Programs for Fiscal Years 2010-2012*; and document provided to CRS in April 2014.

Notes: DA=Development Assistance; GHP=Global Health Programs; NADR=Nonproliferation, Anti-terrorism, Demining, and Related Programs; IMET=International Military Education and Training; FMF=Foreign Military Financing; TI=Transition Initiatives; CARSI=Central America Regional Security Initiative; ESF=Economic Support Fund; INCLE=International Narcotics Control and Law Enforcement.

a. TI country allocations are not yet available for FY2014 or FY2015.

b. CARSI figures only include funds allocated specifically for Honduras. CARSI allocations for Honduras are not yet available for FY2013, FY2014, and FY2015.

c. Complete DOD assistance figures are not yet available for FY2013, FY2014, or FY2015.

State Department and U.S. Agency for International Development

Bilateral Assistance

After several years of increases, U.S. bilateral assistance for Honduras has begun to decline. It fell from $57 million in FY2012 to $52 million in FY2013, and is expected to fall once again to

$41.9 million in FY2014. The Obama Administration has requested $48.2 million for Honduras in FY2015 (see **Table 1**).

The vast majority of the FY2015 bilateral request ($44.3 million) would be provided through the Development Assistance (DA) account, and would be used to support development efforts. Some $15.6 million would be dedicated to strengthening the rule of law, improving governance, supporting decentralization, and fighting corruption in Honduras. Another $10.7 million would be dedicated to basic education programs designed to improve early grade literacy and numeracy, improve the quality of teacher training, and provide learning materials to students. Programs designed to improve food security, strengthen rural markets, and promote renewable energy technologies in communities without access to electricity would receive about $15 million. Additionally, $3 million would be dedicated to environmental programs designed to reduce the vulnerability of extremely poor communities to climate change. The rest of the FY2015 bilateral request ($3.9 million) would be provided through the Foreign Military Financing (FMF) and International Military Education and Training (IMET) accounts to provide equipment and training to the Honduran military.[94]

Transition Initiatives

USAID's Office of Transition Initiatives (OTI) has been active in Honduras since FY2012 and is scheduled to exit the country in FY2015. OTI works in certain conflict-prone countries to provide flexible, short-term assistance designed to support stabilization and political transitions. OTI's program in Honduras is designed to bring security to high violence communities and increase citizen confidence in government institutions. Funding appropriated through the Transition Initiatives (TI) account and allocated to Honduras amounted to $4 million in FY2012 and $3.7 million in FY2013. Funding levels for FY2014 and FY2015 are not yet available.[95]

Central America Regional Security Initiative[96]

The Central America Regional Security Initiative (CARSI) is a regional program that provides Central American nations with equipment, training, and technical assistance to address security challenges. As noted above, CARSI funding is appropriated for all of Central America and then allocated to individual nations or regional programs. Honduras received $13.6 million through CARSI in FY2010, nearly $21 million in FY2011, and $34.1 million in FY2012.[97] Honduras also may have received some additional funding that was allocated to regional programs. It is currently unclear how much FY2013, FY2014, and FY2015 CARSI funding has been allocated to Honduras. Congress appropriated $145.6 million for CARSI in FY2013 and an estimated $161.5

---

[94] U.S. Department of State, *Congressional Budget Justification for Foreign Operations, Appendix 3: Regional Perspectives, Fiscal Year 2015*, April 2014, http://www.state.gov/documents/organization/224070.pdf.

[95] U.S. Department of State, *Congressional Budget Justification for Foreign Operations, Foreign Assistance Summary Tables, Fiscal Year 2014*, May 17, 2013, p.80, http://www.state.gov/documents/organization/208292.pdf; and U.S. Department of State, *Congressional Budget Justification for Foreign Operations, Foreign Assistance Summary Tables, Fiscal Year 2015*, April 18, 2014, p.112, http://www.state.gov/documents/organization/224071.pdf.

[96] For more information on CARSI, see CRS Report R41731, *Central America Regional Security Initiative: Background and Policy Issues for Congress*, by Peter J. Meyer and Clare Ribando Seelke.

[97] U.S. Government Accountability Office (GAO), *Central America: U.S. Agencies Considered Various Factors in Funding Security Activities, but Need to Assess Progress in Achieving Interagency Objectives*, GAO-13-771, September 25, 2013, http://gao.gov/assets/660/658145.pdf.

million for CARSI in FY2014. The Obama Administration has requested $130 million for CARSI in FY2015.

CARSI funding supports a wide variety of activities in Honduras. Some U.S. agencies are using the funds to establish and support specially vetted units and task forces. Equipment and training are provided to Drug Enforcement Administration (DEA) and Immigration and Customs Enforcement (ICE) vetted units and a U.S.-Honduran joint Financial Crimes Task Force in support of complex investigations into drug trafficking, money laundering, and arms and bulk cash smuggling. The Federal Bureau of Investigation (FBI) leads a Transnational Anti-Gang unit designed to interrupt criminal gang activity. A Special Victims Task Force—consisting of vetted members of the Honduran police, the Public Ministry, and U.S. advisors—is looking into high profile violent crime cases, such as the persecution of journalists and members of the lesbian, gay, bisexual, and transgender (LGBT) community. Other CARSI-funded efforts to strengthen Honduran institutions include support for a joint Criminal Investigative School, and border and prison management reforms. CARSI funds are also being utilized to support civil society and municipal government violence prevention programs.[98] At least 40 community outreach centers have been established to provide vocational training, employment resources, and other opportunities for at-risk youth.[99]

Department of Defense

Congress has authorized the U.S. Department of Defense (DOD) to provide several types of foreign assistance,[100] which is funded through annual DOD appropriations measures. While Honduras receives some humanitarian aid, most DOD assistance for the country is focused on counternarcotics efforts. In 2013, for example, several units attached to U.S. Special Operations Command South provided training to the recently established Honduran Naval Special Forces (*Fuerza Especiales Naval*, FEN) unit. The training was designed to strengthen the FEN unit's ability to combat transnational organized crime in and around Honduran waterways.[101] DOD counternarcotics assistance to Honduras amounted to $4.8 million in FY2013. Honduras is expected to receive an additional $3.5 million in DOD counternarcotics assistance in FY2014 and $4.7 million in FY2015.[102]

---

[98] U.S. Embassy in Honduras, "Current CARSI Projects in Honduras," March 6, 2012.

[99] U.S. Congress, House Committee on Foreign Affairs, Subcommittee on the Western Hemisphere, *Advancing U.S. Interests in the Western Hemisphere: The FY 2015 Foreign Affairs Budget*, Prepared Statement of Elizabeth Hogan, Acting Assistant Administrator for Latin America and the Caribbean, USAID, 113th Cong., 2nd sess., April 9, 2014.

[100] For example, Section 2561 of Title 10 of the U.S. Code gives the Secretary of Defense the authority to provide humanitarian assistance. Under Section 1004 of P.L. 101-510, the National Defense Authorization Act of 1991, as amended, DOD can train and transport personnel, construct facilities and certain types of infrastructure, and provide reconnaissance and intelligence analysis services in support of counternarcotics efforts. Under Section 1033 of P.L. 105-85, the National Defense Authorization Act of 1998, as amended, DOD can provide equipment and maintenance support to certain countries (including Honduras) for counternarcotics purposes.

[101] Brian Bird and Gino Rullo, "US Navy Special Forces Help Honduras Form Elite Counter Trafficking Force," *U.S. Southern Command*, February 4, 2013.

[102] DOD data provided to CRS in April 2014.

Millennium Challenge Corporation

The MCC provided Honduras with a five-year, $205 million[103] economic growth compact, which was completed in September 2010. The compact had two components: a rural development project designed to provide farmers with skills to grow and market new crops, and a transportation project designed to improve roads and highways to link farmers and other businesses to ports and major production centers in Honduras.[104] In January 2011, MCC announced that it would not be renewing the compact. Although Honduras passed 16 of 20 indicators on the MCC scorecard, it performed below the median on corruption, which is a "pass-fail" indicator for compact eligibility.[105]

In FY2012, the MCC Board declared Honduras eligible for a so-called threshold program. Threshold programs are designed to help countries identify and address barriers to compact eligibility and constraints to economic growth and poverty reduction. In March 2013, the Board approved up to $15.7 million to support Honduran government efforts to strengthen public financial management and increase the transparency and efficiency of public-private partnerships.[106] A provision of the Consolidated Appropriations Act, 2014 (P.L. 113-76) states that "no country should be eligible for a threshold program after such country has completed a country compact."

Peace Corps

The Peace Corps was active in Honduras from 1963 until January 2012, when the agency pulled all 158 of its volunteers out of the country. Following an in-depth safety and security assessment, the Peace Corps decided to indefinitely suspend its operations. More than 5,700 Americans served in Honduras over the program's nearly four decades in the country, working on projects related to child survival and HIV/AIDS prevention; protected area management; water and sanitation; and business, municipal, and youth development.[107]

Human Rights Restrictions

Many Members of Congress have expressed concerns about the human rights situation in Honduras in recent years, and Congress has placed human rights conditions on security aid to the country since FY2012. Like all countries, Honduras is subject to legal provisions (Section 620M of the Foreign Assistance Act of 1961, as amended, and a recurring provision in the annual DOD appropriations bill) that require the State Department and DOD to vet assistance for foreign security forces, and prohibit funding for any unit if there is credible evidence that it has committed "a gross violation of human rights."[108] There have been additional restrictions on aid

---

[103] The compact was originally for $215 million, but the final $10 million was terminated as a result of the 2009 coup.

[104] Millennium Challenge Corporation (MCC), "Honduras Compact: Raising Incomes, Realizing Dreams" November 3, 2010.

[105] For more information on MCC and how it allocates assistance, see CRS Report RL32427, *Millennium Challenge Corporation*, by Curt Tarnoff.

[106] MCC, *Congressional Budget Justification, Fiscal Year 2014*, p.11, http://www.mcc.gov/documents/reports/report-fy2014-cbj.pdf.

[107] Peace Corps, "Frequently Asked Questions: Peace Corps Operations in Honduras," September 2012.

[108] For more information on these human rights vetting requirements, see CRS Report R43361, *"Leahy Law" Human Rights Provisions and Security Assistance: Issue Overview*, coordinated by Nina M. Serafino.

to Honduras since the enactment of the Consolidated Appropriations Act, 2012 (P.L. 112-74). The act required that 20% of the funds appropriated for assistance to the Honduran military and police forces in FY2012 be withheld until the Secretary of State could report that:

> the Government of Honduras is implementing policies to protect freedom of expression and association, and due process of law; and is investigating and prosecuting in the civilian justice system, in accordance with Honduran and international law, military and police personnel who are credibly alleged to have violated human rights, and the Honduran military and police are cooperating with civilian judicial authorities in such cases.

The 20% withholding requirement did not apply to "assistance to promote transparency, anti-corruption, and the rule of law within the military and police forces." Nor did it apply to assistance provided by the Department of Defense.

Although the State Department issued human rights certifications for Honduras in FY2012 and FY2013, Congress has chosen to maintain restrictions on aid to the country. The Consolidated Appropriations Act, 2014 (P.L. 113-76) modified the human rights conditions for FY2014 by increasing the withholding requirement from 20% to 35%, adding new conditions that must be met, and broadening the exemption so that the withholding requirement does not apply to border security funding. According to the joint explanatory statement accompanying the act,[109] 35% of funds appropriated for assistance to the Honduran military and police in FY2014 must be withheld until the Secretary of State certifies that:

1. the Government of Honduras is reducing corruption including by prosecuting corrupt officials and removing them from office;

2. agreements between the United States and Honduras concerning counter-narcotics operations, including assistance for innocent victims of such operations, are being implemented;

3. the Government of Honduras is protecting freedom of expression, association, and assembly, and due process of law, including in the Bajo Aguan Valley;

4. The Government of Honduras is investigating and prosecuting in the civilian justice system military and police personnel who are credibly alleged to have violated human rights, including forced evictions, or to have aided or abetted other armed groups involved in such acts; and

5. the Honduran military and police are cooperating with civilian judicial authorities in such cases.

In May 2014, more than 100 Members of Congress signed onto a letter to Secretary of State John Kerry expressing their ongoing concerns about the human rights situation in Honduras. The letter calls on Secretary Kerry to pay close attention to the human rights situation, "strictly evaluating U.S. support and training for the Honduran police and military in accordance with the human rights conditions" in P.L. 113-76. It also calls on the State Department and U.S. Embassy in Honduras to "take a consistent and public stance supporting those threatened with human rights

---

[109] The joint explanatory statement is available from the House Committee on Rules at: http://rules.house.gov/bill/113/hr-3547-sa.

abuses, and strongly encourage the investigation and prosecution of those perpetrating crimes, including state agents."[110]

Anti-drug Cooperation

The United States and Honduras have closely cooperated on security issues for many years. Honduras served as a base for U.S. operations designed to counter Soviet influence in Central America during the 1980s, and has hosted a U.S. troop presence—Joint Task Force Bravo—ever since (see the text box, "Joint Task Force Bravo"). Current bilateral security efforts primarily focus on citizen safety and drug trafficking. Many of these activities are funded through CARSI (see "Central America Regional Security Initiative" above).

Over the past decade, Honduras has become a major transshipment point for illicit narcotics. According to the State Department, approximately 86% of the cocaine trafficked to the United States in the first half of 2013 first transited through the Mexico/Central America corridor.[111] While some is trafficked through the air to remote areas that lack state presence, such as the *Mosquitia* region along Honduras's northeastern coast, the vast majority is reportedly trafficked via maritime routes.[112] After making initial landfall in Honduras, cocaine continues on toward the United States on subsequent flights or via sea or overland routes (see **Figure 4**).

> **Joint Task Force Bravo**
>
> The United States maintains a troop presence of about 500 military personnel known as Joint Task Force (JTF) Bravo at *Soto Cano* Air Base in Honduras. JTF Bravo was first established in 1983 with about 1,200 troops who were involved in military training exercises and supporting U.S. counterinsurgency and intelligence operations in the region. In the aftermath of Hurricane Mitch in 1998, U.S. troops provided extensive assistance in the relief and reconstruction effort. Today, U.S. troops in Honduras support activities throughout Central America, such as disaster relief, medical and humanitarian assistance, and counternarcotics operations.

Operation Anvil

In order to reduce the flow of illicit narcotics, the U.S. government has significantly increased its antidrug support to Honduras. As noted above, the DEA maintains a vetted unit, in which DEA agents serve as advisors to select members of the Honduran security forces. From April-July 2012, the United States supported a drug interdiction program known as Operation Anvil. In order to intercept suspected drug smuggling flights, the State Department temporarily transferred six helicopters from Guatemala to Honduras. The helicopters were piloted by Guatemalans and contractors, and carried members of the DEA vetted unit. During the operation, Honduran and

---

[110] Letter from Jan Schakowsky, Member of Congress, et al. to The Honorable John Kerry, Secretary of State, May 28, 2014, http://schakowsky.house.gov/uploads/Letter%20to%20State%20Dept%20re%20Honduras%20Human%20Rights%2005-2014.pdf.

[111] U.S. Department of State, Bureau for International Narcotics and Law Enforcement Affairs, *2014 International Narcotics Control Strategy Report (INCSR)*, March 2014, http://www.state.gov/j/inl/rls/nrcrpt/2014/vol1/222904.htm.

[112] Tim Johnson, "U.S. Won't Send Radar Data to Honduras in Dispute Over Law to Shoot Down Drug Aircraft," *McClatchy Newspapers*, April 1, 2014.

U.S. authorities reportedly interdicted at least 2.25 metric tons of cocaine, arrested seven drug traffickers, and provided a significant deterrent for drug flights entering Honduras.[113]

Operation Anvil also generated considerable controversy, however, as three of the five joint interdiction missions reportedly ended with suspects being killed.[114] A May 2012 incident involving a river boat that left at least four people dead and several others injured has been particularly controversial. While U.S. and Honduran officials assert that the boat was involved in a drug trafficking operation,[115] the boat passengers maintain they were traveling the river for a variety of legitimate purposes.[116] In January 2013, 58 Members of Congress called on the State Department and the Department of Justice to carry out a "thorough and credible investigation" into the May 2012 killings.[117] The agencies' Offices of Inspectors General are currently conducting a joint review of all three incidents that involved the use of deadly force. The joint review will reportedly address pre-incident planning and the rules of engagement, the post-incident investigative and review efforts of both agencies, DEA and State personnel cooperation with post-shooting reviews, and the information the agencies provided to Congress and the public regarding the incidents.[118]

Suspension of Radar Intelligence

In March 2014, the U.S. government reportedly stopped sharing radar intelligence with Honduran authorities. The suspension followed the Honduran government's enactment of a new law authorizing the Honduran air force to shoot down civilian aircraft suspected of engaging in illicit activities. The Obama Administration is reportedly analyzing whether providing information and assistance that would support aerial intercepts is consistent with U.S. law.[119] Radar intelligence sharing with Honduras was previously suspended for four months in 2012 after the Honduran air force shot down two civilian aircraft. It resumed in November 2012, however, after the Honduran government had replaced the head of the air force, revised procedures, retrained pilots, and reportedly signed an agreement not to use U.S. intelligence to "damage, destroy, disable, or threaten civilian aircraft."[120]

---

[113] U.S. Department of State, Bureau for International Narcotics and Law Enforcement Affairs, *2013 International Narcotics Control Strategy Report (INCSR)*, March 5, 2013, http://www.state.gov/j/inl/rls/nrcrpt/2013/vol1/204050 htm#Honduras.

[114] Damien Cave and Ginger Thompson, "U.S. Rethinks a Drug War After Deaths in Honduras," *New York Times*, October 12, 2012.

[115] U.S. Department of State, Office of the Spokesperson, "Taken Question: Drug Enforcement Administration Investigation Honduras," June 6, 2012.

[116] See: Annie Bird and Alexander Main, *Collateral Damage of a Drug War: The May 11 Killings and the Impact of the U.S. War on Drugs in La Moskitia, Honduras*, Center for Economic and Policy Research & Rights Action, August 2012, http://www.cepr net/documents/publications/honduras-2012-08.pdf.

[117] Letter from Henry C. "Hank" Johnson, Jr., Member of Congress, et al. to The Honorable John Kerry, Secretary of State, January 30, 2013.

[118] U.S. Department of Justice, Office of the Inspector General, "Ongoing Work: Drug Enforcement Administration," May 2014, http://www.justice.gov/oig/ongoing/dea htm.

[119] Tim Johnson, "U.S. Won't Send Radar Data to Honduras in Dispute Over Law to Shoot Down Drug Aircraft," *McClatchy Newspapers*, April 1, 2014.

[120] Damien Cave, "As U.S. Shares Intelligence with Honduras, Other Antidrug Aid Stays Frozen," *New York Times*, November 27, 2012.

Figure 4. Cocaine Trafficking Routes in Honduras

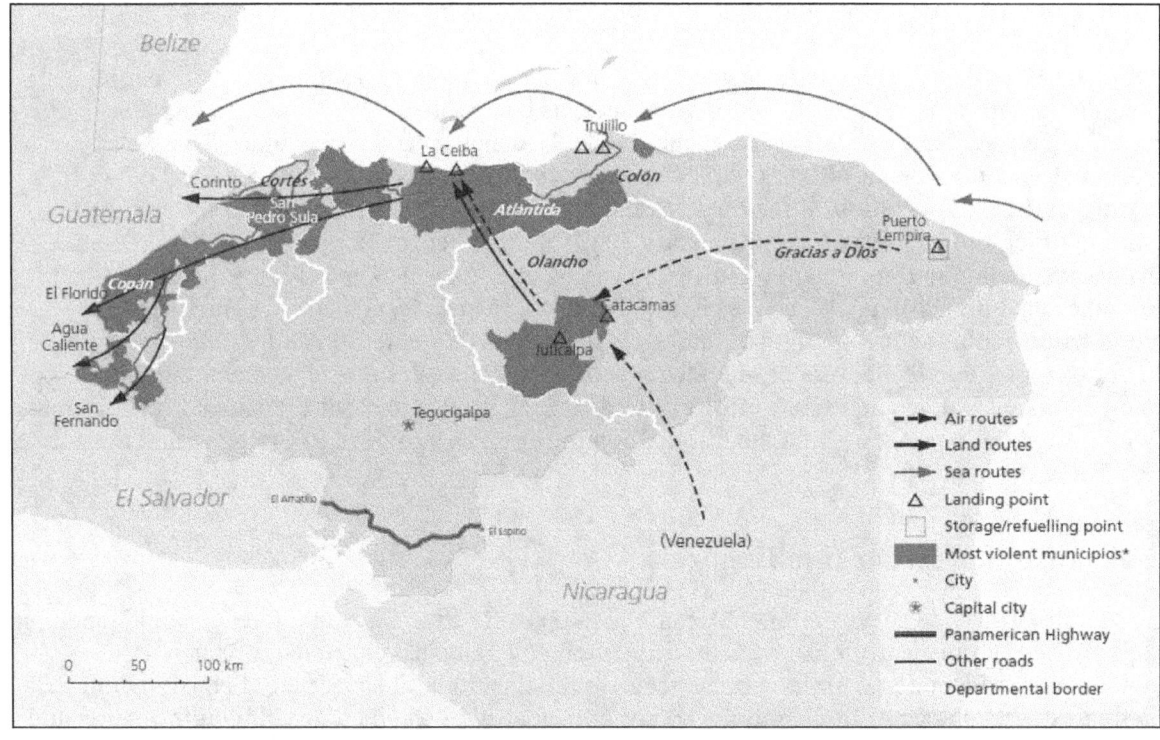

Source: U.N. Office on Drugs and Crime (UNODC), *Transnational Organized Crime in Central America and the Caribbean: A Threat Assessment,* September 2012, p.38, http://www.unodc.org/documents/data-and-analysis/Studies/TOC_Central_America_and_the_Caribbean_english.pdf.

Kingpin Sanctions

Over the past two years, the U.S. Treasury Department's Office of Foreign Assets Control (OFAC) has labeled several Honduran individuals and organizations as Specially Designated Narcotics Traffickers pursuant to the Foreign Narcotics Kingpin Designation Act, freezing any assets they may have had under U.S. jurisdiction and prohibiting U.S. citizens from conducting financial or commercial transactions with them.

- On April 9, 2013, OFAC announced the designation of José Miguel "Chepe" Handal Perez, his wife, his father, and various businesses under their control. OFAC asserts that Handal is the head of a Honduran drug trafficking organization that facilitates the movement of multi-ton shipments of cocaine between Colombian sources and two Mexican trafficking organizations, *Los Zetas* and the *Sinaloa* cartel.[121]

- On May 31, 2013, OFAC designated *Los Cachiros*, a Honduran drug trafficking group that is reportedly headed by Javier and Leonel Rivera Maradiaga and controls 90% of the clandestine airstrips in Honduras and Guatemala.[122] OFAC

---

[121] U.S. Department of the Treasury, "Treasury Designates Honduran Traffickers," Press Release, April 9, 2013.

[122] U.S. Department of the Treasury, Office of Foreign Assets Control, "Specially Designated Nationals Update," May 31, 2013; "Lobo: Seguridad Debe Conocer de Los Cachiros," *La Prensa* (Honduras), July 9, 2013.

---

implemented further sanctions on Los Cachiros on September 19, 2013, designating seven individuals and five businesses tied to the group.[123]

- On April 9, 2014, OFAC designated Carlos Arnoldo Lobo ("El Negro Lobo"), who reportedly worked with Colombian suppliers to transport cocaine north for Mexican, Guatemalan, and Honduran drug trafficking organizations, including the Sinaloa cartel and Los Cachiros.[124] The Honduran authorities had arrested Lobo in March 2014, and extradited him to the United States on drug trafficking charges in May 2014. Honduras had never extradited a Honduran citizen prior to Lobo.

Commercial Ties

U.S. commercial ties with Honduras have increased significantly since the early 1980s. In 1984, Honduras became one of the first beneficiaries of the Caribbean Basin Initiative (CBI), a unilateral U.S. preferential trade arrangement providing duty-free importation for many goods from the region. In the late 1980s, Honduras benefitted from production-sharing arrangements with U.S. apparel companies for duty-free entry into the United States of certain apparel products assembled in Honduras. As a result, *maquiladoras*, or export-assembly companies, flourished, mostly concentrated in the north coast region. The passage of the Caribbean Basin Trade Partnership Act in 2000, which provided Caribbean Basin nations with North America Free Trade Agreement (NAFTA)-like preferential tariff treatment, further boosted the *maquila* sector. Trade relations have expanded most recently as a result of the Dominican Republic-Central America-United States Free Trade Agreement (CAFTA-DR), which significantly liberalized trade in goods and services after entering into force in April 2006.[125]

Trade and Investment

Despite a significant decline in bilateral trade in the aftermath of the global financial crisis, total merchandise trade between the United States and Honduras has increased nearly 33% since the implementation of CAFTA-DR in 2006; U.S. exports to Honduras have grown by 43% and U.S. imports from Honduras have grown by 22% (see **Figure 5**). Since a large portion of imports from Honduras entered the United States duty free prior to implementation of the agreement, analysts had predicted that CAFTA-DR would lead to a relatively larger increase in U.S. exports. Total two-way trade amounted to $9.8 billion in 2013, $5.3 billion in U.S. exports to Honduras and $4.5 billion in U.S. imports from Honduras.[126] In addition to textile and apparel inputs, discussed below, top U.S. exports to Honduras in 2013 included refined oil products, electric machinery, heavy machinery, cereals, and plastics. Top non-apparel imports from Honduras included insulated wire, edible fruit, gold and other precious metals, seafood, and coffee.[127]

---

[123] Embassy of the United States Tegucigalpa, Honduras, "Treasury Targets 'Los Cachiros' Drug Trafficking Organization in Honduras," Press Release, September 19, 2013.

[124] U.S. Department of the Treasury, "Treasury Targets Honduran Maritime Drug Trafficker Carlos Arnoldo Lobo," Press Release, April 9, 2014.

[125] For more information on CAFTA-DR, see CRS Report R42468, *The Dominican Republic-Central America-United States Free Trade Agreement (CAFTA DR): Developments in Trade and Investment*, by J. F. Hornbeck.

[126] U.S. International Trade Commission (USITC) data as presented by the *USITC Interactive Tariff and Trade DataWeb*, May 2013.

[127] U.S. Department of Commerce data, as presented by *Global Trade Atlas*, accessed May 2014.

Similar to previous trade arrangements, CAFTA-DR has provided substantial benefits to the textile and apparel assembly industry in Honduras. Textiles and apparel accounted for over 56% of U.S. imports from Honduras in 2013. Likewise, textile and apparel inputs, such as yarns and fabrics, accounted for more than 24% of U.S. exports to Honduras.[128] However, the Trans-Pacific Partnership (TPP),[129] a proposed Asia-Pacific regional trade agreement, has the potential to alter the textile trade. The agreement could allow Asian apparel producers to export clothing to the United States duty-free, eliminating much of the advantage now enjoyed by Honduran and other Western Hemisphere apparel producers. Additionally, U.S. exporters of textile and apparel inputs could face increased competition in Honduras and elsewhere in the Western Hemisphere if the TPP were to allow apparel manufacturers to use yarn and fabric made anywhere in the TPP region and still enjoy preferential access to the U.S. market.[130]

Figure 5. U.S. Trade with Honduras: 2004-2013

In billions of U.S. dollars

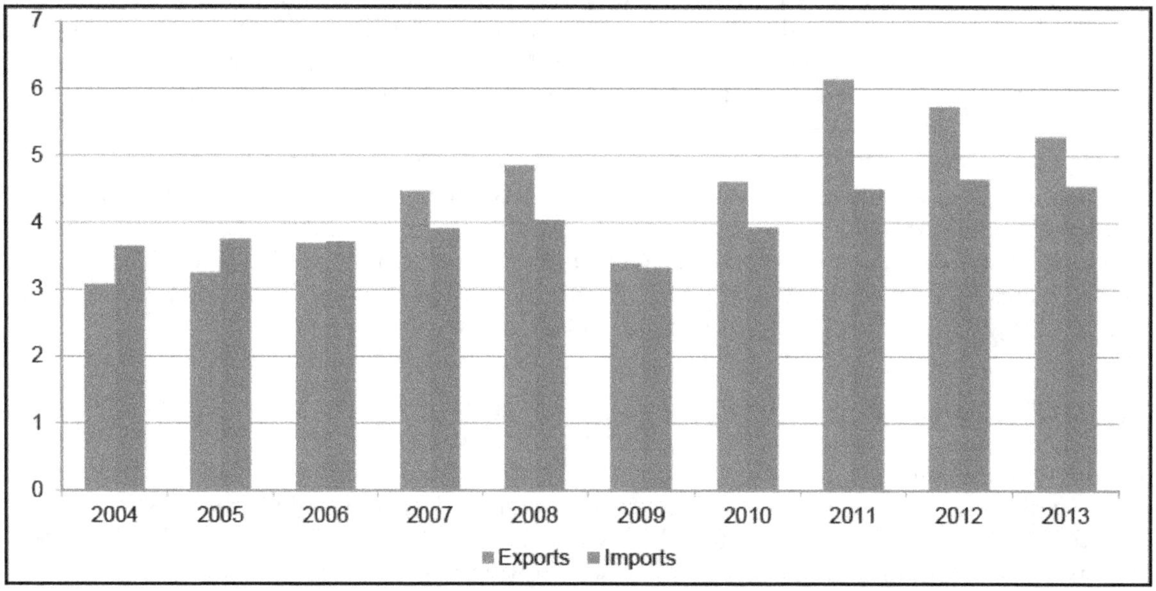

Source: CRS presentation of U.S. Department of Commerce data obtained through the U.S. International Trade Commission, *Interactive Tariff and Trade DataWeb*, accessed May 2014.

U.S. foreign direct investment in Honduras has also grown since the implementation of CAFTA-DR. The total stock of U.S. foreign direct investment in the country amounted to $881 million in 2012 (the most recent year for which data are available), an increase of about 12% from $787 million in 2006.[131] According to the State Department, relatively low labor costs, proximity to the U.S. market, and the Caribbean port of Puerto Cortés make Honduras attractive to investors. At

---

[128] Ibid.

[129] For more information on TPP, see CRS Report R42694, *The Trans-Pacific Partnership (TPP) Negotiations and Issues for Congress*, coordinated by Ian F. Fergusson.

[130] CRS Report R42772, *U.S. Textile Manufacturing and the Trans-Pacific Partnership Negotiations*, by Michaela D. Platzer.

[131] U.S. Bureau of Economic Analysis, "Balance of Payments and Direct Investment Position Data," accessed May 2014.

the same time, high levels of crime, a weak judicial system, corruption, low levels of educational attainment, and poor infrastructure hamper investment.[132]

Labor Rights

Despite these increases in trade and investment, some in the United States and Honduras have expressed concerns about the implementation of CAFTA-DR. Labor rights provisions have received particular attention. According to the State Department, Honduran law provides for unionization and collective bargaining, but places a number of restrictions on those rights and frequently fails to enforce labor protections. In 2013, "antiunion discrimination continued to be a serious problem....Employers commonly threatened to close unionized factories and harassed or dismissed workers seeking to organize. They also fired leaders with impunity soon after unions were formed to prevent the union from functioning." Moreover, "there was credible evidence that some manufacturing factory employers continued with impunity to blacklist employees seeking to form unions" and "there were several cases in which union leaders were threatened with violence."[133]

In March 2012, the American Federation of Labor and Congress of Industrial Organizations (AFL-CIO) joined with Honduran trade unions to file a petition with the U.S. Department of Labor. The petition asserts that the government of Honduras has failed to effectively enforce its labor laws and meet its obligations under CAFTA-DR, and calls on the U.S. government to engage Honduras on these issues to ensure future compliance.[134] The Department of Labor's Office of Trade and Labor Affairs (OTLA) accepted the petition in May 2012, initiating a review of up to 180 days to determine the accuracy of the charges and issue a public report with its findings and recommendations. In November 2012, OTLA announced that it needed to extend the review period.[135] Although two years have passed since the petition was accepted, OTLA has yet to report its findings.

Migration Issues

Migration issues are central to the U.S.-Honduran relationship as an estimated 1 million Hondurans reside in the United States—some 600,000 of whom are believed to be undocumented.[136] Migration from Honduras to the United States is primarily driven by high levels of poverty and unemployment, though the security situation in Honduras has increasingly

---

[132] U.S. Department of State, Bureau of Economic, Energy and Business Affairs, *2013 Investment Climate Statement – Honduras*, February 2013, http://www.state.gov/e/eb/rls/othr/ics/2013/204655 htm.

[133] U.S. Department of State, Bureau of Democracy, Human Rights and Labor, *Country Reports on Human Rights Practices for 2013*, February 27, 2014, pp.25-26, http://www.state.gov/documents/organization/220663.pdf.

[134] American Federation of Labor and Congress of Industrial Organizations (AFL-CIO) et al., *Public Submission to the Office of Trade & Labor Affairs (OTLA) under Chapters 16 (Labor) and 20 (Dispute Settlement) of the Dominican Republic-Central America Free Trade Agreement (DR-CAFTA)*, March 26, 2012, http://www.dol.gov/ilab/reports/pdf/HondurasSubmission2012.pdf.AFL-CIO.

[135] U.S. Department of Labor, Bureau of International Labor Affairs, "Dominican Republic-Central America-United States Free Trade Agreement; Notice of Extension of the Period of Review for Submission 2012-01 (Honduras)," 77 *Federal Register* 66870, November 7, 2012.

[136] U.S. Department of State, Bureau of Western Hemisphere Affairs, "U.S. Relations with Honduras," March 24, 2014.

---

played a role as well.[137] Given the persistence of these conditions in Honduras, polling indicates that over 36% of Hondurans who still live in their home country would like to emigrate.[138] Honduras has joined with other Central American nations to lobby the U.S. Congress in favor of comprehensive immigration reform,[139] and President Hernández has reportedly stated that the United States has "a moral obligation" to approve such legislation.[140]

In addition to relieving social pressure, emigration plays an important role in the Honduran economy. Remittances from migrant workers abroad are the largest single source of foreign exchange for Honduras. They more than tripled between 2003 and 2008 before declining in 2009 as a result of the global financial crisis and U.S. recession, which left many Honduran immigrants unemployed. Remittances have since recovered, however, growing by 14% between 2010 and 2012 to reach $2.9 billion (equivalent to about 16% of Honduras's GDP).[141] The United States and Honduras have sought to maximize the development impact of remittance flows with the Building Remittance Investment for Development Growth and Entrepreneurship (BRIDGE) Initiative that was launched in September 2010. Under the initiative, the United States and Honduras partner with financial institutions to leverage the remittances they receive to obtain lower-cost, longer-term financing in international capital markets and fund investments in infrastructure, public works, and commercial development.[142]

Deportations

Deportations to Honduras have increased significantly over the past decade. Nearly 37,000 Hondurans were deported from the United States in FY2013, making Honduras one of the top recipients of deportees on a per capita basis.[143] Increasing deportations from the United States have been accompanied by similar increases in deportations from Mexico, a transit country for Central American migrants bound for the United States. Honduran policy makers have expressed concerns about their country's ability to absorb the large volume of deportees, as it is often difficult for those returning to the country to find gainful employment. Individuals who do not speak Spanish, who are tattooed, who have criminal records, and/or who lack familial support face additional difficulties re-integrating into Honduran society. In addition to these social problems, leaders are concerned that remittances may start to fall if the current high rates of deportations continue.

Some analysts contend that U.S. deportations of individuals with criminal records have exacerbated gang and security problems in Honduras and other Central American countries. U.S. Immigration and Customs Enforcement (ICE) does not provide receiving countries with the

---

[137] "Masiva Fuga de Hondureños por Inseguridad y Desempleo en el País," *El Heraldo* (Honduras), June 16, 2013; Cindy Chang and Kate Linthicum, "Nation Sees a Surge in Asylum Seekers; Critics are Wary of Fraud as 'Credible Fear' Filings from Central Americans Jump," *Los Angeles Times*, December 15, 2013.

[138] ERIC-SJ, January 2014, op. cit., p.14.

[139] "Central America Will Lobby as One for US Migration Reform," *Latin News Daily Report*, February 14, 2013.

[140] José Meléndez, "Entrevista. EPN Rompe Ausencia de México en CA," *El Universal* (Mexico), April 2, 2014.

[141] Inter-American Development Bank (IDB), Multilateral Investment Fund (MIF), "Remittances to Latin America and the Caribbean," 2013, http://www5.iadb.org/mif/en-us/home/knowledge/developmentdata/remittances.aspx.

[142] U.S. Department of State, Office of the Spokesman, "U.S. BRIDGE Initiative Commitments with El Salvador and Honduras," September 22, 2010.

[143] U.S. Department of Homeland Security, Immigration and Customs Enforcement, "FY2013 Removals by Departed to Country," 2014.

---

complete criminal records or gang affiliations of deportees, however, it may provide them with some information regarding deportees' criminal histories and gang affiliations when specifying why the deportees were removed from the United States. In January 2014, the State Department and the Department of Homeland Security signed an agreement to expand a Criminal History Information Sharing (CHIS) program to Honduras and other Central American nations. The CHIS program previously has been used to share information on certain criminal deportees with Mexican law enforcement officials. About 45% of the Hondurans deported from the United States in FY2013 were removed on criminal grounds.[144]

Temporary Protected Status[145]

Since Hurricane Mitch struck Honduras in 1998, the U.S. government has provided temporary protected status (TPS) to allow eligible Hondurans—who may otherwise be deported—to stay in the United States. Originally slated to expire in July 2000, TPS has now been extended 11 times. The most recent TPS extension came on April 3, 2013, when the Secretary of Homeland Security announced that the United States would continue to provide TPS for an additional 18 months, expiring on January 5, 2015 (prior to this extension, TPS would have expired July 5, 2013). According to the *Federal Register* notice on the most recent extension, the Secretary of Homeland Security determined that the extension was warranted because "there continues to be a substantial, but temporary, disruption of living conditions in Honduras resulting from Hurricane Mitch, and Honduras remains unable, temporarily, to handle adequately the return of its nationals."[146] An estimated 64,000 Hondurans residing in the United States benefit from TPS.[147]

Trafficking in Persons

According to the State Department's 2013 *Trafficking in Persons Report*, Honduras is primarily a source and transit country for men, women, and children trafficked for the purpose of commercial sexual exploitation and forced labor. Many victims are subjected to forced prostitution in urban and tourist locales such as Tegucigalpa, San Pedro Sula, and the Bay Islands. Destination countries for trafficked Honduran women and children include El Salvador, Guatemala, Mexico, and the United States. There are also foreign victims of commercial sexual exploitation in Honduras, most having been trafficked from neighboring countries. Additionally, there have been reports of rural families leasing out children for forced labor, and urban gangs coercing young males to transport drugs or act as hit men.

The State Department maintains that Honduras does not fully comply with the minimum standards for the elimination of trafficking; however, it notes that the government is making significant efforts to do so. As a result, Honduras is considered a so-called "Tier 2" country. The State Department report recognizes the Honduran government for passing a comprehensive anti-trafficking law in 2012 that prohibits all forms of trafficking, includes sufficiently stringent punishments, and establishes more robust victim protections. Nevertheless, the report asserts that

---

[144] Ibid.

[145] For more information on TPS, see CRS Report RS20844, *Temporary Protected Status: Current Immigration Policy and Issues*, by Ruth Ellen Wasem and Karma Ester.

[146] U.S. Department of Homeland Security, "Extension of the Designation of Honduras for Temporary Protected Status," 78 *Federal Register* 20123-20128, April 3, 2013.

[147] "Gobierno Anunciará Hoy Ampliación para el TPS," *La Tribuna* (Honduras), June 3, 2013.

the Honduran government's services for victims remain inadequate, and its efforts against forced labor remain weak. The State Department's recommendations for Honduras include increasing efforts to investigate and prosecute trafficking offenses, and ensuring dedicated funding to provide specialized services and shelter to trafficking victims.[148]

Author Contact Information

Peter J. Meyer
Analyst in Latin American Affairs
pmeyer@crs.loc.gov, 7-5474

---

[148] U.S. Department of State, Office to Monitor and Combat Trafficking in Persons, *Trafficking in Persons Report 2013*, June 19, 2013, http://www.state.gov/j/tip/rls/tiprpt/2013/index htm.